D1240514

JOMO KENYATTA

Father of Harambee

JOMO KENYATTA

Father of Harambee

by
Egara Kabaji

Illustrated by
Andrew Akhonya

Sasa Sema Publications
Nairobi

Copyright © 2000 Egara Kabaji
Illustrations copyright © 2000 Andrew Akhonya
Cover painting copyright © 2000 Dorothy Migadde

ISBN: 9966-951-01-6

Published by
Sasa Sema Publications Ltd.
P.O. Box 13956 Nairobi
Second printing 2002

All rights reserved.
No part of this publication may be reproduced, stored in a retrieval
system or transmitted in any form by any means without permission
in writing from the publishers.

Printed by
English Press
P.O. Box 30127 Nairobi

CONTENTS

PREFACE

A good book, like a good relationship, is a collaborative effort. There is only one name on the cover of this book, but many people helped me write it. Even more than most authors, I was favoured with gifts of time, and the expertise and insights of others for which I am eager to express my gratitude.

Because I am not a historian, I am especially indebted to the work of historians on Jomo Kenyatta. Masinde Aseka's *Jomo Kenyatta: A Biography*, G. Arnold's *Kenyatta and the Politics of Kenya* and Murray Brown's *Kenyatta* were particularly helpful.

Other books that have provided insights into the

personality of Jomo Kenyatta included: Oginga Odinga's *Not Yet Uhuru*, Bildad Kaggia's *The Roots of Freedom*, Andrew Morton's *Moi: The Making of an African Statesman* and Jules Archer's *African Firebrand: Kenyatta of Kenya*.

Kenyatta's own *Facing Mount Kenya* and *Harambee! 1963-1964* were also very valuable. On much of the information about Kenyatta's cultural background I am indebted to *The Southern Kikuyu Before 1903*, Volumes 2 and 3, by L.S.B. Leakey.

Several editors read and improved upon the manuscript. I thank Dr. Godfrey Muriuki of the University of Nairobi for reading the manuscript and lending his expertise in a few important corrections. Dr. Kakai Wanyonyi of Kenyatta University was particularly generous with his knowledge of Kenyan history and society. Zarina Patel gave valuable contributions from her knowledge of Kenyan history. Dr. Edwin Nyutho of the University of Nairobi helped deepen the authenticity of the text. John Sibi-Okumu and Kaari Njeru read the manuscript carefully and made many improvements.

In the writing of this book, I have received from Lila Luce the kind of cooperation and support that is an author's most elusive reward. No one has committed more time and care to the book than her. She read each draft with a childlike attitude and remained patient and helpful. There are many other people who lent credibility to this book, among them is the entire team at the Sasa Sema offices.

In any book of this nature, it is easy to veer off course on the road from conception to publication. I was lucky, as there was always somebody nearby to point me back in the right direction.

This was a particular problem here because I was dealing with Jomo Kenyatta, a man revered and loved by many but also loathed by an equal number. Mine was not to demonise Kenyatta nor to make him out to be an angel. I have tried to present Jomo Kenyatta as a great Kenyan with all his strengths and weaknesses. I hope that after reading this book, you will not just condemn or applaud Kenyatta unquestioningly, but you will understand what made him act as he did.

CHAPTER ONE

THE LAND OF MUMBI AND GIKUYU

 A long time ago there lived a hard-working woman called Wambui. Her home was on Ng'enda Ridge, near Thika town, and she was the mother of two sons.

Every morning while it was still dark, Wambui joined the other women as they walked down the hills to their small plots.

They sang songs in praise of hard work, and ridiculed the lazy people in society. Wambui often started a song and the rest would join in as they worked. She would also tell them stories about their people's origins, about irresponsible husbands, about destructive wives and many more things.

"A long time ago…" she started one story, drawing the attention of the other women, "there lived a mean man. The man used to sneak into the kitchen and drink the children's milk…" The women working near her listened keenly, as they loved Wambui's stories.

"One day," Wambui continued, "the children got together and chased him from the home. From that day men have become more careful."

"No, no, we still have some who steal from their wives!" interjected one of the women.

"Well," replied Wambui, "if you know of any in this village, tell us and you will see what we will do to him!" Everyone broke into a fit of laughter.

In the evening, Wambui prepared supper, *irio* with vegetable soup, and she sat with her two sons as they waited for their meal to get ready.

"Mama," said Kamau, "today I met the ogre

from the story you told us yesterday!"

"No, Son. Where would you see an ogre?"

"I did see it, where the women work making pots."

"What had you gone to do there, and I told you never to go there!"

Men and boys were never allowed to go to

the place where they make pots. The women said that if they came to where they were working, the pots would crack, and the women would have to start their work all over again. Kamau knew very well that he was not supposed to go near the place. But he wanted to see what would happen if he went there! Would a pot really break?

Kamau was a loving, well-meaning boy, but he had a mischievous streak in him, and loved to convince the other boys to do things that they were not supposed to do. Sometimes they sneaked into a neighbouring farm to steal sugarcane. Sometimes they tried to scare other people's goats!

"Please tell us another story," he pleaded.

"First promise me you will not go to the place where they make pots again."

"I promise, Mama."

"That's good. Now, which story shall it be tonight, my sons?" asked his mother.

"Tell us the story of Mumbi and Gikuyu again," pleaded Kamau's little brother, Kungu.

"My sons, that is what I will do," said Wambui. She stirred the steaming *irio* in the pot, as her two sons waited expectantly.

"In the beginning *Ngai*, *Mwene Nyaga*, Owner of Ostriches, made a big mountain which he called *Kirinyaga*, The Place of Ostriches."

"And Ngai called out to Gikuyu, who was the first man!" put in Kamau.

"And he took him to the top of the mountain!" added Kungu.

Wambui put another piece of wood on the fire. "Yes, my sons," said Wambui. "And then what did Ngai tell Gikuyu?"

Just then, the boys' father, Muigai wa Kungu, came into the hut and greeted his family. "Are you well, mother of Kamau?" he began.

"Yes, everything is good here," replied Wambui.

"I have brought some meat to add to the food tonight," said the father.

"This is good," replied Wambui. "It will help the boys become strong."

Muigai wa Kungu turned to Kamau and asked him, "My son, are you learning how to be a man?"

Kamau answered, "Yes, baba, I am going to be a strong man."

His father laughed loudly. "My son, a strong man is always ready to help others when they need it. Remember, one finger does not kill a louse."

"I do, baba! I am always helping others!"

This was one of the important lessons a boy had to learn. Kamau helped his father and uncles build houses for neighbours who were sick. He, together with some of the other boys of his *rika*, his age-group, helped care for the animals of older people who had lost their children. And he knew that if he or his family, were ever in trouble, all the others would come to help.

Kamau grew up with this sense of strong community spirit, and it was the seed of the idea of *harambee*, working together in unity.

When their father went out, the mother and her two boys finished the story of Gikuyu and his wife, Mumbi, and their nine daughters.

CHAPTER TWO

THORNS
AND DARK FOREST

 Early one morning Kamau was woken up by loud noises. He turned around to ask his mother about the noise, but she was not on her bed. He rushed out of their hut and saw a crowd of people in the homestead. His mother was there with the other mothers, and they were all weeping and wailing.

He ran towards his mother. "Mama, why are you all crying?" he asked.

"Wooooiiii!" she sobbed.

"What is it, Mama?" Kamau asked, clinging onto her dress.

"You have been left an orphan, my son. We are doomed. Your father has died."

Before long, his little brother, Kungu, fell ill and Kamau lost his only brother, right after losing his father.

After Kamau's father died, their lives changed. Kamau's father had a brother and, as was the custom, this brother took Wambui as his wife. Wambui gave birth to another son, Ngengi, and so Kamau had a baby brother again.

But Kamau's uncle did not treat Wambui and Kamau well. He was cruel to them, and finally Wambui decided to return to her parents' home with her children.

Long before dawn the next morning, Wambui woke up Kamau, whispering softly to him, "My son, get up. We have to go on a journey."

Kamau obeyed his mother, and before he knew it, he was on the footpath out of the village with his mother by his side. His baby brother, Ngengi, was tied onto his mother's back. In the distance they could hear the howl of a hyena.

"Mama, where are we going?" Kamau asked.

"We are going to a place where there is plenty to eat," she replied.

"Do they have many goats there?" he asked her, finally.

"Yes, my son, they have many goats and sheep."

They followed the narrow footpath, under tall trees and through giant climbers. Wambui knew that her son was scared of the forest, and every now and then she would check to see that Kamau was close to her.

As the day became brighter, Wambui pointed out birds, trees and herbs, teaching Kamau their names. When Kamau spotted a

snake or other animal, Wambui would tell him about that one, too.

Wambui pointed to a small green shrub hiding in the shade. "See this little plant? It is *ndonga*," she said. "It fights poison. If someone is bitten by a snake, find this plant and rub the root over the place where the person was bitten."

"I will, Mama," replied her son, as he studied the *ndonga* plant. "Look at this one, Mama," he cried, pointing to a tree growing just beyond the *ndonga* shrub. "That is a strange one!"

"Yes, that one is called *munderendu-waitu*. It is a very rare tree. If you ever find its seedling anywhere, make sure you do not uproot it."

"Look at its flowers!" Kamau cried, running over to examine it in detail.

"Kamau, don't run off the footpath," called his mother.

"Aaiii!" cried the boy, as one immense vine

caught him. Its long
sharp thorns had
stuck him in several
places.

"Mama,
how do I
get out of
here?" he
cried.

His mother came over to where he was.
"And now where have you put yourself?!" she
scolded him teasingly, after seeing that he had
not been hurt. She carefully pulled him free
from the thorns, and they were able to
continue on their way.

When they arrived at Wambui's parents'
home, the sun was high in the sky. Everyone
gave them a warm welcome. Wambui explained
what had happened, and her brothers provided
her with a hut for herself and her sons.

Kamau found a flock of happy, playful boys
among his new-found cousins. They explored

together up and down the near-by streams and sometimes they hunted birds and small animals.

As they tramped through the forest, Kamau liked to tell jokes and entertain his cousins.

"I throw an arrow into an open plain. Who am I?" he asked them, posing one of the riddles his father had taught him long ago.

"I know that one!" cried one small boy. "Your eye!" he said, jumping up and down. And he was right. An eye does indeed reach very far into the distant plains.

"Eh, but do you know this one?" challenged Kamau again. "I stand in the midst of spears and am not harmed."

The other boys remained silent for a while. Some tried to guess, but finally they gave up. "What is it, Kamau?"

"My tongue!" shouted Kamau triumphantly. "It's enclosed by my sharp teeth!"

"Aaah! That's a good one!" exclaimed the others.

Life was pleasant. There was plenty of food and lots of fun. But one day, as the boys were fishing down stream, they heard loud noises of people wailing. The sounds were coming from their home. Kamau stood up and listened. A shiver ran down his spine. He had heard this sound once before, the time when his father died. He ran up to the homestead. There were people crowding around his mother's hut. Kamau rushed inside.

His mother was lying on a mat. She wasn't moving. He knelt down close to her and touched her forehead. "Mama," he said, nervously. "Mama... wake up... wake up, Mama..." His voice began to tremble. There was no movement from his mother.

It began to dawn on this little boy that he was losing his mother.

"Wooiii!" he wailed, as he realised that the

worst had happened. His beloved mother was dead.

Kamau didn't know what to do. He ran off into the forest and stayed there among the tall trees for long periods. He ran back to the hut. His aunts tried to get him to eat but he refused. They tried to comfort him, but he just ran back into the forest and stayed there for a whole day at a time.

His mother's death was a turning point in his life. He had lost his father, and now his mother. He was an orphan, and "the eldest" of his little family of two. He was about twelve years old. He would now have to provide food for himself and his four-year-old half brother. Kamau would have to be the decision-maker now for both of them.

It soon became clear to Kamau that he and Ngengi were not welcome in their mother's parents' home any more. Now that their mother had died, they no longer belonged there, and Kamau had to return with his little

brother to the home of their fathers in
Ng'enda, where they belonged.

After bidding the family members goodbye,
Kamau and Ngengi set off on their journey to
return to Ng'enda Ridge. Kamau was no
longer afraid, and held Ngengi's hand as they
trudged through the thick undergrowth.

By the time they had crossed three rivers, it
was the middle of the
day and they were
hungry and tired.
They sat down next
to a big tree to rest.
Kamau heard birds
singing and looked
up into the trees.

High above them he could see some ripe fruits
hanging down from the branches. But they
were too far to reach.

Kamau opened his small bag and got out
his catapult. He picked up a small stone and
positioned it in the sling, then aimed at one of

the fruits. He released the sling and...pop!...the fruit dropped out of the tree.

He picked it up, smelled it, then tasted it, and then gave some of it to Ngengi.

By late afternoon, they had arrived in Ng'enda. The relatives, sorry to hear about their mother, Wambui, gave them an extra hut where they could stay.

At Ng'enda, Kamau began to grow into a tall, strong teenager. But it was a hard time for him. He had to do all the work, because he had neither mother nor father there. He took care of the animals and helped the other boys and men to hunt and build. Not only did he have to do the work of boys, he even had to do the work that was done by women and girls. He would sweep the house every morning, cook for Ngengi and himself, and fetch water and firewood.

Nevertheless, he laughed a lot, entertained people with jokes and, like his mother before him, he was a great storyteller. People liked him so much that they even gave him a special nickname. Kamau had started wearing a brightly-coloured beaded belt which was called a *kinyata*. As people saw him walking in the fields wearing his beaded belt, they would say "There is *kinyata!*" This nickname pleased him, and many years later he adopted it as his official name.

Kamau was not afraid of hard work, and he was not even too proud to do women's work. But he was thinking of the future. He had to find a life for himself independent from his father's family's home. He decided the best thing would be to join his grandfather some distance away in a village called Muthiga.

CHAPTER THREE

MAGIC

Kungu wa Magana was a *mundo mugo*, a medicine man and a wise seer for the community. He could heal many illnesses with herbs and magic and he could foretell the future. His knowledge and wisdom was so great that people came from the surrounding villages and even from far away for advice on governing, war and drought.

"My Grandson, you are welcome in my home," Kungu said to the boy when he arrived. "It is high time you started to learn the art of the *mundu mugo*. Watch tomorrow, and see what I do."

The next morning, an old man came to Kungu wa Magana's home.

"Grandfather!" called Kamau, running into his grandfather's hut. "Someone has come!"

"Yes, Kamau. Tell him to sit down in the courtyard and I will come. And bring my stool," he added.

Kungu went into his first wife's hut, where he kept all the things he needed for his art. When he came out he was carrying his goatskin mat and a string bag holding his herbs and powders, his gazelle horn charm, and, most importantly, his divining gourd filled with hundreds of *mbugu*.

Each medicine man, during the days of his initiation into the arts of magic and medicine, had a special gourd made for him by an elder, more experienced medicine man.

Inside this magic gourd were hundreds of *mbugu* , different little objects, which had special meanings for the medicine man. There were rare stones from high up on the mountain, leaves and twigs from special plants, pieces of bones, bits of skin, seeds, even cowrie shells from far away. Each of these *mbugu* helped give the medicine man information to diagnose illnesses, to foretell the future, and to make wise judgements on matters in the community.

Kungu approached the place where the old visitor was waiting. He put his mat down on the ground and took his stool from Kamau.

Kamau wanted to see and hear everything and started to kneel down next to his grandfather. But Kungu motioned Kamau to leave them alone. Reluctantly, Kamau sat down in the shade of a tree and watched from a distance.

The relationship between a medicine man and his patient was confidential. Sometimes an illness is brought about by the person's bad behaviour.

The medicine man needed to know what the person did in order to solve the problem. In privacy, the patient could feel free to say anything, knowing his medicine man would never tell anyone else.

For a few moments, Kungu sat across the old man, looking intently at him. He was reading his eyes for signs of how he could help him. Kungu then placed his gourd carefully between his knees, and, after praying to Ngai, he poured out some thirty or forty of the *mbugu* onto the mat.

"Take a handful of the *mbugu* and pour them here," Kungu instructed his patient. The old man gathered many of the little objects into his hands, and then poured them out again onto the goatskin.

Kungu studied the little stones, shells and bones. "*Mbugu ya igana na igiri...one hundred and two mbugu objects...*" he sang.

Kungu then spoke to the old man quietly, telling him what he saw, and asking him questions. In his wisdom, he knew that most illnesses were caused partly by matters of the heart and soul. The old man replied to Kungu's comments and questions, and they talked together in low tones for some time. Finally, Kungu looked up and reached for one of his powdered herbal mixtures.

"Take this in *ucuru*, porridge," he instructed his patient.

The old man got up slowly and went away. Kungu knew that, once the problem was solved, the old man would come back with a small animal or other prize as payment for the medicine man's services. Indeed, a few days

later the old man returned to Kungu's home,
happily carrying a young goat. Kungu accepted
the animal, happy that, once again, he had
helped someone solve a difficult problem.

In the afternoons, Kamau accompanied his
grandfather on journeys to some distant area.
He was proud that his grandfather let him carry
his string bag containing his magic gourd with
all the *mbugu* in it.

Little by little Kamau learned how to
recognise the trees and herbs which could be
used as medicine. He even helped his
grandfather prepare the mixtures for his patients.
It was like magic. His grandfather always knew
what was wrong, and he always knew how to
cure it, if it could be cured.

If his grandfather's art seemed like magic,
Kamau soon learned about another art that
seemed to have even greater magic. But the
magicians of that particular art were strange
people.

Kungu had once told his grandson about a
prophecy made by Mugo wa Kibiru, who had

been a great medicine man long before. This wise man had foretold that one day some strangers would come their land. Their bodies would be light coloured, like the bellies of frogs, and they would be dressed like butterflies. Moreover, they would bring with them a huge snake, which would have as many legs as a centipede!

"And his prophecy was a warning," continued Kungu, "that we should not fight these people, because they would be carrying killing sticks which would spit out fire. And we should never let them get near our homes because they would try to take our land. However," he concluded, "these people are to bring great wealth."

At the time that Kungu was telling Kamau about this prophecy, some of it had already come true. The strange people had started appearing about the time that Kamau was born. They were light coloured and did indeed dress like butterflies. They carried sticks that spat out fire and killed people. And while he was still a small boy, these strange people started creating that huge snake with many legs. It was the railway!

The only question was, would they also try to take the land?

One day, word went around that one of these strange people was in the area. Kamau was curious. He wanted to see what a person would look like if they were coloured like the belly of a frog!

A large group of people had gathered in a neighbouring village to meet the newcomer. The visitor was almost white. The prophecy had been true.

This strange white man was making marks in the ground with a stick. As he made each mark, he would say a word.

"*Kuria*, to eat," he said as he wrote the letters in the ground with his stick.

The white man explained that the marks he

made stood for words and ideas. Kamau was astonished to learn that ideas could be communicated with marks in the ground made with a stick. The marks the man had just made were the same as when someone said "*kuria*"!

"Where can I learn this magic?" asked Kamau, as he watched the strange person making another mark in the ground.

"You can learn these things, and more, in the mission school at Thogoto," the man replied. "That is where I teach. Would you like to come to the school?"

This man was very friendly, and Kamau did not hesitate in saying 'yes.' The stranger spent some time with Kamau showing him things about the magic of writing and reading.

It seemed to Kamau that these people had medicine that was even more magical than his grandfather's. Not only could they cure some of the things that Kungu said were incurable, but they also had this other magic of making marks in the ground to communicate ideas.

Young Kamau was so excited about this new

magic, that it took him some time to fall asleep that night. He kept on imagining how wonderful it would be to know how to read and write. "I will go to this school," he resolved to himself.

CHAPTER FOUR

SCHOOL

 Kamau woke up very early. It was a cold misty morning and the birds were singing their melodious tunes. The cocks had already announced the dawn of a new day and the hyenas had retreated into the thick forest.

Although members of the family tried to persuade him not to go off to the mission school, Kamau had made up his mind. He had to learn this new magic.

He knew he would miss his home, and sadly said goodbye to his grandfather and to everyone else. As he set off, he turned in the direction of

Kirinyaga, and quietly whispered a prayer.

When Kamau arrived at Thogoto late in the day, it was very hot. He had walked the whole day, and he and his clothes were all covered with dust.

The year was 1909, and Kamau was a tall, confident teenager. The master at Thogoto School could see in his brilliant eyes a rare determination and yearning to learn.

"Hey, boy, what do you want here?"

"I have come to learn how to read and write," Kamau answered.

"What is that hanging on your shorts?" demanded the master.

"It is my machete," Kamau replied.

"Who have you come to fight?" the master asked.

"Nobody, Sir, it is just for my self-defence."

"Let me have it. We can't have you savages bringing in your war activities here." With that, the master admitted Kamau into the school.

Kamau learned how to read and write English and he also picked up Swahili. This made him very happy. A whole new world was opening up for him.

However, Kamau learned many things at Thogoto besides reading and writing. When a boy was admitted into the school, he was expected to be a new convert to Christianity.

Every morning the boys were woken up by a loud gong. By sunrise, they would be seated in the church.

"God of Abraham, Jacob and Isaac," the missionary would begin, "We thank you for everything you have given us..."

Who was this? Kamau asked himself. He

wondered whether this God was like Ngai. Did he know Ngai? Where was the dwelling place of this God? What had he done for them that they should thank him?

In that school, Kamau was baptised into the new religion, and that meant thinking and acting in new ways, and even getting a new name. When he was baptised, he chose the name "Johnstone" for his Christian name. He put together the names of two of the people he most admired from the Bible, St. John the Baptist, and the disciple, Peter. Peter means 'stone' in Greek. And so he became known as Johnstone Kamau.

Kamau also learned that not all British men were good like the first one he had met near his home. Some of the teachers wanted to mislead the boys into hating themselves as black people and hating African traditions. As a result, the boys sometimes lost their self-confidence, their creativity and their sense of belonging to the African society.

One day, one of the stricter masters made an

announcement to all the boys.

"You have learned enough about reading, and now you will start learning how to do

something useful. You will now learn the art of carpentry, so that you can make tables and chairs."

The boys turned to one another in amazement.

"Yes!" the master continued. "Carpentry is a very useful activity. People will always need furniture and cabinets. And, you never know, you might be lucky and make a chair that will be used by Her Majesty the Queen!"

The boys walked away from this assembly muttering among themselves in low tones.

"Why does the teacher treat us this way?" whispered one of the boys.

"The man thinks we are so stupid…"

"Well, let me tell you," Kamau interrupted, "these people are up to no good. They want us to be their servants!"

Kamau began to realise that Kenya was ruled by these white people from Britain. He learned that this was called colonialism. Colonialists are people who come to another country and take it over as if it were their own country. It was because of colonialism that people like this master could get away with such rude and disrespectful behaviour.

"How can we be treated like this and grow into men?" one boy whispered to Kamau.

"Let us endure this inhumanity for the moment," Kamau urged him, "so that we can learn their ways, and be prepared to defeat them in the future!"

"What I hate is the man's arrogance," complained another. "He thinks his ways are better than ours!"

"We shouldn't allow them to brainwash us into hating our culture," advised Kamau. "We have a wonderful culture. Let us be proud of it!"

Kamau stayed at Thogoto School long enough to learn the magic of reading and writing. He learned to be a good carpenter, and earned his keep making cabinets and furniture. He also worked as a houseboy. Then, when he was about 18, he left Thogoto and returned home.

"Reading and writing are wonderful magical things," he said to himself, "but they are not enough, as long as these outsiders rule Kenya."

CHAPTER FIVE

THE FIGHT FOR LAND

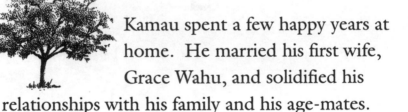Kamau spent a few happy years at home. He married his first wife, Grace Wahu, and solidified his relationships with his family and his age-mates.

But then something terrible happened. Kamau learned that some of the people in neighbouring villages had been forced off their land. The British government had taken the land from Kenyans and given it to British farmers.

Moreover, the British government had announced that all the land in Kenya was to belong only to Britain. This meant that all

Kenyan families, who had lived on their land for generations, had their land taken away from them. The rest of Mugo wa Kibiru's prophesy had now come true!

Later, the colonial government made their policy completely racist. People did not have to come from Britain to get some of the land, they just had to be white. Some white people came from Canada, Australia and South Africa to take up farms in Kenya.

Land is very important in African culture because contact with the soil is part of African worship. Moreover, land is the source of livelihood. By keeping Africans off their own land, the colonial government was keeping them poor. With no other way of making a living, Africans were forced to take low-paying and demeaning jobs working under the colonialists.

Kamau was forced to look for work in the big city. But he was luckier than most. He was quick and clever and charming. Also, his education opened the door to a job as a meter reader for the Nairobi City Council. Later he

was promoted to the rank of inspector at the
Nairobi Water Works. With his hard-earned
money, Kamau built a house at home.

It was now the 1920's, and Kamau was a
striking man, tall and towering, with a rugged,
bearded face. He had intense, intelligent eyes.
He made himself even more imposing by going
about in a big American cowboy hat and big
brown boots.

He still wore his trademark *kinyata* belt, and
people started calling him by his old nickname,
Kinyata. Kamau liked the name and encouraged
people to use it. It was changed to "Kenyatta,"
and that is how he began to be known as
"Kenyatta."

Kamau, now Kenyatta, was charming and
persuasive and he could express his ideas well.
He always dressed smartly and went to cinemas
and horse races with influential people. He
spoke English and Swahili and he found that the
ability to read and write helped in the fight for
justice.

As people became more bitter and restless

about the colonial government, Kenyatta began
to be seen as a symbol of progress with an ability
to lead. He found himself being one of the
central figures in discussions about how bad
things were and how to change them. He even
turned his house into a small shop where, in the
evenings, people would gather to buy a drink
and talk.

"They have taken our land, and are forcing
us to work on their farms," complained one
man.

"And even on the little land they have left
us, they want to tell us what to plant!" cried
another.

"Yes," added a third man, "I wanted to
plant coffee and they have outlawed it!"

"Soon they will demand our wives!" quipped
the first one, to a chorus of laughter.

"No, no," replied Kenyatta, "this is no
laughing matter. They are trying to keep us

poor."

"Yes," agreed another, "they do not want us to plant cash crops, because they do not want us to make our own money."

"We may have to fight these people; they are too stupid to listen to reason," concluded Kenyatta.

Many Kenyans, both Africans and Asians, had already been demanding justice and equality from the British for many years. Now Kenyatta and others were calling for justice in a second great wave of resistance. People were beginning to feel that the time was now ripe to confront the oppressors more directly.

Many groups were formed among Asians as well as Africans, all trying to resist the British colonial government. One of these groups was the Kikuyu Central Association.

The Kikuyu Central Association decided it was time to send an envoy to England, the land of the colonial government. They wanted to press for justice and equality. They wanted Africans to have a hand in the governing of

Kenya. And they also wanted Africans to have the opportunity to own land again.

Kenyatta was one of the leaders of the Kikuyu Central Association, and he was considered to be the best choice as envoy to England.

Kenyatta agreed to go. He thought that he might be able to do some good. It was also a great opportunity to get to know the oppressor better.

It was a cold, wet and foggy day in March 1929 when Kenyatta arrived in London. The city seemed grey all over, filled with tall stone buildings and many cars, and many people hurrying through the streets. People were not friendly; they did not even bother

to greet each other in the streets as Africans did. He missed sunny, friendly Kenya.

However, he got to know a number of brilliant Africans and they gathered their strength to fight for independence of African nations. There was Kwame Nkrumah, who later became the president of Ghana. There was Paul Robeson, the African American singer and writer. And there was Ladipo Solanke, a Nigerian freedom fighter. Kenyatta's interaction with these and others exposed him to methods of advocacy for peaceful and non-violent revolution against colonial governments.

Kenyatta was also interested in finding a form of government which encouraged the idea of common sharing, something similar to the traditional African systems of governments, and which could work in Africa.

He decided he had to study human nature itself, and how different civilisations governed themselves over the centuries. He went to a university and studied anthropology, the science of human civilisations and cultures.

Kenyatta especially wanted to explain African culture to Europeans. One of the reasons colonialism was so hard to fight is that many non-Africans did not understand African culture. Kenyatta wanted to show those people that they were wrong to think that European culture and religion were better than African culture and religion. For these reasons he decided to write a detailed study of Kikuyu culture.

"African culture is beautiful," he explained, "and the rest of the world should know about it. I want to put the record straight and demonstrate how colonialism is destroying a system that has worked for centuries."

Before he published the book, Kenyatta thought about changing his name. He felt that, as the author of this book, he should be known only by African names.

"I have thought about the name, *njomo*," he confided to a friend, "that is, the Kikuyu term for a spear or two-edged sword."

"Yes," replied his friend, "it would fit your sharp wit and piercing vision!"

Finally, the name was shortened to 'Jomo,' and that is how he became known as Jomo Kenyatta. Sometimes *njomo* is translated as "burning spear," and Kenyatta is sometimes called that, too.

Kenyatta called his book *Facing Mount Kenya.* It was published in 1938. The book created a stir, and Kenyatta became a respected writer and lecturer. He received many invitations to give lectures interpreting African culture to Europeans. The book also strengthened the idea that British colonialism in Africa was wrong, and in the long run, it helped the movement toward independence of African nations.

In the year 1939 the Second World War broke out, involving all of Europe and large parts of Asia and Africa. There was no chance to return to Kenya at that time, and Kenyatta continued to write articles and books, and had many discussions about how to achieve independence for colonised nations.

In particular, Kenyatta questioned the fact that Africans were being forced to join a war that concerned only Europeans. Africans could not gain anything from this war, and yet they were sent to far-off places to carry supplies, to fight, and sometimes to die. They worked under very harsh conditions. Many Africans died and those who returned received no reward for their services.

Although his main energies were poured into these deep concerns, he also found time to enjoy the social life of London. He knew how to dress smartly, laughed and joked and told great stories, and so he had many friends. He also became a favourite of the English girls.

Eventually he fell in love with Edna Grace Clarke and married her in 1942. They lived together in an English village, and he made friends at the local pub there.

"Well, well," started one fellow pub customer, "you must be from Africa."

"Yes, I am," said Kenyatta.

"And what is your name, Sir?"

"Jomo Kenyatta."

"Eh? Jumbo? Like the elephants! You have lots of elephants down there in Africa, don't you?"

"Yes, we do," Kenyatta replied.

And so Kenyatta became known as 'Jumbo' in the English village.

Kenyatta had gone to England to find a way in which Africans could share in the governing of their country. He had gone to get back the land that had been taken from them. But after he spent some time in London, he realised that these things, even if granted, would not be enough. Kenya had to become totally free from England.

For some time people in Kenya had been asking Kenyatta to return home and lead them. Kenyatta, himself, began to realise that the struggle could only be won from within the country, and that he could not help very much as long as he stayed in England. As soon as the Second World War ended, Kenyatta decided to return home.

CHAPTER SIX

WAR

The Second World War ended in 1945. Kenyatta came back to Kenya soon afterwards, burning with ambition, knowledge, and energy. He had become a leader of status not only among his own people, the Gikuyu, but also throughout the whole of the colony of Kenya. Wherever Kenyatta went, big crowds of excited Kenyans received him.

"Eeeeeh Comrades!" Jomo Kenyatta cried joyfully, holding his walking stick high in the air above him. There was wild applause! The women trilled!

He still wore his colourful beaded *kinyata* belt, and a thick leather lumber jacket. "Didn't we go to fight in their war? Didn't they tell us that they would give our land back?"

Kenyatta's tall, imposing figure and large bearded head commanded authority. His piercing eyes electrified the audience.

"Eeeeeeaaaaaah! Have they given it back?"

The crowd roared.

"How can we agree to be squatters in our own country? How can they force us to work for them?"

The sounds of shouting and screaming were deafening! Kenyatta was a dynamic and dramatic speaker. He had a hypnotic effect on his audiences. People loved him.

Kenyatta spoke to the people in Swahili. Sometimes he used Kikuyu phrases so that the Kikuyu elders would not think that he had forgotten his mother tongue after all those years in Europe! He was eloquent in both languages, and when it was appropriate for him to speak in

English, he spoke beautifully.

The colonial government had banned public meetings, but Kenyatta was not cowed. He moved around to all the Kenyan provinces, talking to people and declaring that the colonialists should give back the land, repeal the oppressive laws, and let Kenyans govern themselves. He became a national leader.

In 1947 India became independent from British colonialism. Here was a large country that had been under the power of the British for more than a hundred years. This was a great boost to anti-colonial movements everywhere, because it proved that freedom from colonialism was possible. It encouraged the people of Kenya.

The end of the Second World War also brought back the Kenyans who had been sent to fight in Asia. These men, angry and smart—and knowledgeable about guns—began to organise their own war at home. They called themselves "The Forty Group," after the year 1940, the year they came of age together.

Kenyatta himself did not join in the armed conflict, and publicly distanced himself from this group. However, he had already seen that persuasion alone might not be enough.

Perhaps it would take confrontation on all sides, even physical force, to send the British away.

"Any means that will wake up the colonialists should be used," he said.

The members of the Forty Group were convinced that only an armed struggle would succeed at liberating Kenya. The British government had a strong military force at their command: police and soldiers, guns and vehicles.

The Forty Group had to use other kinds of weapons. Their strategy was to use surprise and hiding and trickery. By careful planning and an intimate knowledge of the countryside, they could cause a lot of problems for the colonial government, even without many guns and soldiers. This is what is called guerrilla warfare.

`The most intense fighting took place from bases hidden in the thick forests around Mount Kenya and the Aberdare Mountains, in the central part of the colony.

Members of the Forty Group attacked police stations and farms owned by British settlers. Any Africans who supported the British cause were considered to be enemies, and members of the Forty Group attacked them, too. They planned surprise attacks, popping out of the forest all of a sudden, and they came to be known as *Mau Mau*.

As the movement grew, many women risked their lives over and over again carrying food, medicines and guns to the warriors in the forest. Some women even joined the fighters in the forest.

In 1952 the Mau Mau war intensified. The colonial government met violence with violence. Homes of suspected members of the *Mau Mau* were destroyed. Freedom fighters were hunted

down, and murdered when they were caught.
Crops were burned in the fields, often the food
of whole villages full of innocent people. In
some places, police patrolled the villages all day
and all night.

The colonial government formed a network
of spies among the villagers to inform on illegal
activities. Each village was placed under the
command of a "homeguard."

Homeguards worked for the British
colonialists. They turned in anyone they
suspected of supporting the Mau Mau
movement, and became, themselves, targets of
Mau Mau anger.

On 20 October 1952, the British Governor
of Kenya declared a state of Emergency. This

gave the government enormous powers to imprison people. Thousands of Kenyans were taken out of their villages and rounded up into outdoor prisons where the hot sun would beat down on them all day. Families were broken up, some to never see their loved ones again. Many people were beaten, tortured, and killed. Kenya had entered a difficult period.

Although Kenyatta had always made it very clear that he was not part of the Mau Mau movement, the colonial government didn't believe it.

"Are you the leader of Mau Mau?" cried a voice from one of the crowds of listeners.

Kenyatta smiled roguishly. He had been waiting for that question. "Mau Mau?" he asked with a twinkle in his eyes. "What is that?"

The crowd roared with laughter. No one living in Kenya at that time could not know what Mau Mau was. However, the government could never pin him down on whether he was really a part of it.

In any case, Kenyatta had such a following

among the people of Kenya, that the colonialists felt they would be safer if he was in the hands of the colonial government. They decided to arrest him.

CHAPTER SEVEN

DETENTION

 It was very early in the morning when the soldiers arrived at Kenyatta's home. They expected to find him asleep, but they were surprised. He was waiting for them, sitting up in his brown leather lumber jacket!

"You are late!" he said to them mischievously. He knew they were coming for him. Not much happened in Kenya without Kenyatta knowing about it.

Contemptuously, he held out his hands for them to handcuff him. "Do you need all these soldiers to arrest one person?" Kenyatta asked them sarcastically. He had no respect for this show of force.

He was led to a land rover and taken away. He and five other freedom fighters were put on trial. They were Bildad Kaggia, Paul Ngei, Achieng' Oneko, Kung'u Karumba and Fred Kubai. The trial lasted five months.

The colonialists wanted Kenyatta and the others to be out of touch with all their supporters, and so they held the trial in Kapenguria, a remote town in the northern part of Kenya.

There was no courthouse, and an old schoolhouse was used as a courtroom. There were no railroads, telephones or hotels, and only a very bad dirt road leading south to Nairobi. It was very hard for the six prisoners to get friends there, and for journalists to cover the events. Even so, friends and journalists came.

"Do you admit that you incited people to violence?" the judge asked.

"No, your Honour," said Kenyatta.

"Are you not the one who has been addressing public meetings asking people to arm themselves and destroy the property of the settlers?"

"No, your honour, it is the government that has brought violence to us. The government has thrown people out of their farms, closed their schools and limited their freedom of worship and movement," Kenyatta explained.

"Where are the *Mau Mau* troublemakers now?"

"You must know better than I; you are the ones who have been chasing them," said Kenyatta.

Kenyatta and the five others were found guilty of causing violence and unrest in the land. Once the judge announced the verdict, the defendants had a chance to speak, and they agreed to let Kenyatta speak for all of them.

"On behalf of my colleagues," Kenyatta began, "I wish to say that we are not guilty, and we do not accept your findings."

Many witnesses had lied in court. Kenyatta

knew that those witnesses had been bribed by the colonial government to give false testimony against them.

"This case," continued Kenyatta, "from our point of view, has been so arranged as to make scapegoats of us in order to strangle the people of Kenya." Kenyatta looked around the courtroom at all the people, enemies as well as friends. "We look forward to the day when peace shall come to this land and that the truth shall be known that we, as African leaders, have stood for peace."

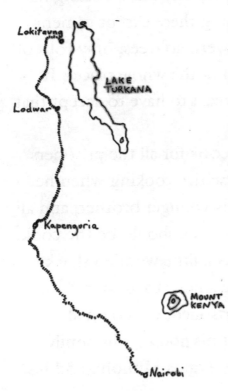

The "Kapenguria Six" were sentenced to seven years hard labour in a remote place in northern Kenya. The colonial government feared

Kenyatta so much that he was sentenced to be held in restriction for the rest of his life. They were led out one by one, handcuffed. A few days later they were flown to Lokitaung, a small outpost in harsh desert wasteland near the Sudan and Ethiopian borders.

When he arrived at Lokitaung, Kenyatta was beaten and forced to wade through a poisonous cattle dip, submerged entirely until it stung his eyes. There was nothing there except cement block houses. There were no trees, only rolls of barbed wire surrounding the whole place. It would sink anyone's heart to have to accept that as home.

Kenyatta was the cook for all the prisoners. He had had a lot of practice cooking when he was a boy caring for his younger brother, and all the prisoners agreed that he should be the cook. The prison kitchen was a little wooden shack with a chimney for the smoke to go out.

While he was imprisoned, the colonial government destroyed his house. His family, including his new wife, Ngina Muhoho and his new-born daughter, were left without adequate shelter. He knew they were suffering, but there was nothing he could do.

Kenyatta and each of the other prisoners were known by numbers, not by names. The prisoners were forced to address an British man as *afande*, Sir.

There were many harsh rules. When a prisoner broke one of these rules, he was put into a hole in the ground that was covered with steel. With no trees or shade, this hole became a hot oven in the day, and the prisoner would bake

in there with no water or fresh air. Kenyatta was once kept in the hole for five days, and when he was brought out, he could not walk. He had almost died from heat and thirst.

Even though they were in detention, the prisoners were sometimes able to get books brought in by visitors. Kenyatta read about the religions of the world, including Hinduism, Buddhism and Confucianism. He also read Gandhi's thoughts on non-violent resistance as a means to achieve peaceful change. It was Gandhi's leadership that brought about the independence of India from British colonialism a few years earlier.

Through occasional visitors, Kenyatta was able to get word out to the press. Also he was interviewed by journalists, some friendly, some hostile.

"Why can't you stop those *Mau Mau* bandits from destroying property?" asked one journalist.

"I am not behind *Mau Mau* activities," Kenyatta replied. "And now that I am here, how do you suppose I would have any influence at all?"

In 1960 Kenyatta was still in detention, but he was transferred to Lodwar. All this time, the people of Kenya could not forget Kenyatta and kept him close to their hearts. They clamoured for his release every day:

> *Tuvute kamba twende Lodwar!*
> *Aye, tuvute kamba twende Lodwar!*
>
> *Let's pull together, and go to Lodwar!*
> *Let's free our leader from prison!*

Fellow leaders visited Kenyatta at Lodwar over and over again, bringing him books and news. When he heard about the independence of Ghana in 1957, he was very encouraged. "If it can happen in Ghana," he thought to himself, "it can happen here."

CHAPTER EIGHT

UHURU!

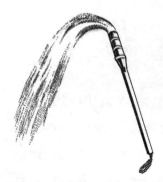

Those in the colonial government had thought that people would forget Kenyatta if they imprisoned him. This never happened. Rather, the name "Kenyatta" became a magical name throughout the land. Leaders from all over the country insisted that Kenyatta was their leader. They pressed for his release.

One of the most vocal supporters of Kenyatta's release was another activist, Oginga Odinga. He coined the slogan *Uhuru na Kenyatta!* which was echoed all over the country: Independence with Kenyatta!

Ambu and Lila Patel organised a campaign to free Kenyatta. They were close to Kenyatta and had looked after his wife during Kenyatta's detention. They also hid Mau Mau fighters in their house in Nairobi.

People also formed trade unions. Makhan Singh organized a very effective strike among the dock workers in Mombasa. Kenyans were causing the British so many problems that finally the British had no choice. They had to give in to the demands of the people.

Kenyatta was freed in 1961. He was about seventy years old. He was flown home to a great welcome-home gathering of 30,000 joyful people. There he was, the same beloved Kenyatta, tall burly bearded figure in his leather jacket, beaded cap and *kinyata* belt.

"*Baba wa taifa !* Father of the nation!" they cried. This was the beginning of the end of the long, terrible journey.

"Uhuru!" he cried, waving his fly-whisk high in the air above him.

"Eeeeeehh! Uhuru!" roared the happy crowd.

It was time to negotiate independence from Britain and Kenyatta joined these efforts. Finally the Kenyan leaders and the British government agreed that Kenya would become an independent country in two big steps.

The first step was for Kenya to govern itself. This was *madaraka*, internal self-government. In May, 1963, there was a national election. Kenyatta was elected to be the new nation's Prime Minister.

One of the ideas he raised in his election speech was the idea of *harambee*, or pulling together.

"Workers use this word when they have a joint task to perform, such as pulling a log or pushing a wagon," he told the people. "It means, let's all work together. Get up and go!"

And ever since, *harambee* has been an important concept to describe all Kenyans working together to build their country in unity.

And then, on the first of June 1963, Kenya was granted internal self-government. Every year thereafter Kenyans have celebrated Madaraka Day as a national holiday.

However, this status of having internal self-government was not yet total independence. Kenya was still a state under the Queen of England, and could not yet be considered a fully independent country among all the nations of the world.

So the second step would be to achieve total *uhuru*, independence from Britain. But before this could happen, many preparations were required. A constitution had to be decided upon. And some decisions had to be made about land.

Kenyatta had stressed in his election victory speech that no land would be taken away from people.

"Every community will retain their land. Everyone, the Abaluyia, the Maasai, the Kalenjin, the Mijikenda, everyone. It will be theirs to manage."

But how should the newly independent country treat the European settler community? They, after all, were the oppressors for many years. And many of them still kept large farms in Kenya and wanted to stay in the country.

In August of 1963, Kenyatta met with white European settlers in the Nakuru Town Hall. These farmers were very nervous as they walked into the Town Hall.

One tall man who had a farm near Nanyuki muttered to his friend, "Will this Kenyatta throw us off our farms?"

"Eh, if that happens, I can't stay here. What would I do without my farm?" said his companion.

"But Kenya is our home! How can we leave just like that?" the other answered.

As they were settling in their chairs, their new Prime Minister walked onto the stage. He raised his fly whisk, and the sounds died down. Kenyatta leaned over his walking stick and started speaking.

"Kenya will soon be an independent country, and you are all part of it," he began. "You may think that I hate Europeans. I do not. I only hate what colonialism did to Kenya."

Kenyatta shifted his weight on his walking stick, looking around the room. "We want you to stay here and farm the land. Our country needs your experience. Continue to farm your land and you will find the government will support you in your efforts."

Kenyatta watched his audience, and tried to gauge their mood. They were quiet. Were they with him? Suddenly he straightened up from his walking stick and called out, "Harambee!"

His audience looked at him in stunned

silence. They knew what the word meant, but they were not sure what Kenyatta was trying to tell them.

"Harambee!" he cried again, swinging his fly whisk high in the air above him.

The tall farmer from Nanyuki raised his arm in the air. "Harambee!" he shouted.

One woman who had a farm in the Rift Valley stood up. Throwing her fist into the air she called "Harambee!" She loved Kenya. It was her country. "Let's stay and support our new government!" she cried.

Soon several others joined in the call to work together to build the country. "Harambee!" they also cried.

Kenyatta was happy. He had prayed for this reconciliation between erstwhile enemies.

Now, at the dawn of a new nation, it seemed that everyone would work together no matter what their backgrounds.

Many of the white settlers decided to leave. Some returned to England. Others went to South Africa or Zimbabwe (it was called Rhodesia in those days), but many others, loving Kenya and trusting Kenyatta, decided to stay and continue to farm.

Independence Day had been scheduled for the evening of 11 December of that year. Kenya would actually be granted independence at the stroke of midnight. And so the date 12 December 1963 would be the first day of the independent country. That would be the day when power would be officially transferred from England to the new government of Kenya.

As the day approached, thousands of Kenyans began to stream into the capital city of Nairobi. They came from all over the country. Even some of the Mau Mau fighters emerged from the forests to attend the ceremonies. They had never felt safe as long as the British were in power.

Dance troops came from all over the country to perform that evening. They came with their musical instruments from the four compass points of the country, from Turkana, from Giriama, from Kisii, from Lamu. Kenyatta loved to watch these colourful, exciting expressions of Kenyan culture.

Then, exactly at midnight, the lights went out and there was total darkness. For a few breathless moments, thousands of people waited in the pitch black stadium. Then, all of a sudden, the lights came on and there was the official flag of the Republic of Kenya flying in the wind! The black, red, green and white colours were dancing against the night sky for all to see.

Everyone cheered and roared with happiness! "*Uhuru! Uhuru!*" they cried.

Brightly coloured fireworks exploded up into the sky. Pow! Pam! The official marching band struck up the notes of Kenya's national anthem:

UHURU!

Eee Mungu nguvu yetu
Ilete baraka kwetu
Haki iwe ngao na mlinzi
Na tukae na undugu,
amani na uhuru
Raha tupate na ustawi. . .

There was whistling, stamping of feet and
screams of joy soaring into the night sky above!
Kenyatta rose up from his seat, and came to
stand there in front of the crowds. People cried
and screamed! "Uhuru! Kenyatta!" they cried.
Then he waved his fly whisk slowly back and
forth above his shoulder.

"Ladies and gentlemen..." Prime Minister

Kenyatta began. The sounds died down, as people waited to hear what he had to say. There was soon almost total silence in the whole large stadium.

"It is with great pride and pleasure that I stand before you today. This is the greatest day in Kenya's history, and the happiest day of my life."

People cried and clapped. Kenyatta went on to talk about the great importance in setting up a new government in the right way. Finally, he added,

"Now, my words to the people of Kenya. Many people may think that, now there is *Uhuru*, now I can see the sun of Freedom shining, riches will pour down like manna from Heaven. I tell you there will be nothing from Heaven. We must all work hard, with our hands, to save ourselves from poverty, ignorance and disease. Only we can save ourselves. Nobody else can."

The moment Kenyatta finished his first speech as leader of an independent nation, there

was a silence. Then the clapping started, and
with the clapping, screams of joy, and stamps
and trills. People started dancing. Even
President Kenyatta danced with them, and all of
this went on through the night.

Across the new nation, similar celebrations
were taking place. In the stadium in Mombasa
thousands of people cried out joyfully when
when the British flag came down. This was part
of the meaning of *uhuru*: no longer would a
foreign flag fly above Kenyan soil. Indeed, an
independent nation had been born!

CHAPTER NINE

HARAMBEE

 Once Kenya was an independent nation, Kenyatta devoted all his energies to unifying the country. *Mzee*, respected elder, as he began to be called, realised that the most important thing was to hold Kenya together as one nation. And he found many, many obstacles on the way.

Kenya decided to have no connection at all with Britain. On 12 December 1964, Kenya was declared *jamhuri*, a republic, totally independent from Britain. And that is why today we have Uhuru Day on the same day as Jamhuri Day.

Kenyatta knew that Kenya had the potential of being an important agricultural nation in Africa through the development of its tea, coffee, sugar, sisal, cotton and pyrethrum. He knew that the country would always be able to feed itself.

But the people had to have land. With land, they had the opportunity to farm. It was important to settle landless people in farms, so that they could contribute to this great agricultural wealth.

At the time of independence, many people had no land. And because of colonialism, many of the British settlers' families had vast farms in some of the best agricultural land in the country.

Some of these settlers had decided to leave Kenya. Kenyatta arranged to have the government buy their land at fair prices, and offer it to landless Kenyans at affordable prices which could be paid for in instalments.

This decision raised a lot of criticism. Some critics said that the land was not being distributed fairly. The best land, they said, was going to Kenyatta's close friends and family. They said that everyone had fought for freedom, and they thought that Kenyatta was not being fair.

Other critics said that the British settlers should not have been paid for the land.

"*Mzee*, the land was stolen from us, and we should take it back without paying a penny," they insisted. "How can we buy what was stolen

from us?"

"*Mzee*, we have already paid by fighting for this land!" insisted others. "Why should we pay again?"

Kenyatta did not agree. "We can no longer blame the colonialists for all our problems," he said. "We have to forgive those who oppressed us," he explained. "We must forgive, but never forget."

"*Mzee*, is this freedom, to let our oppressors keep our land?" they demanded.

"Do you think we have achieved our freedom," Kenyatta responded, "if someone can walk into a shop and say 'this is my property' or go onto a farm and say 'this is my farm' and then it is theirs?" Kenyatta turned and looked at his listeners.

"Is that freedom? No. We did not fight for freedom in order to oppress others."

But everywhere he turned there were threats to unity.

In the north-eastern part of the country, a vast semi-desert land, lived several thousand

Kenyans who belonged to ethnic groups of Somali descent and language. The Kenyan Somalis began to assert their right to secede from Kenya, and become part of Greater Somalia.

Kenyatta could understand their point of view. After all, they were Somali in their culture and language, and felt closer to the Somalis in Somalia. But Kenyatta was concerned first and foremost with the unity of the country.

If the Kenyan Somalis decided to leave Kenya to form their own country, then other groups of people might think about doing the same. Perhaps the people from the Kenyan coast would decide to secede from Kenya. Maybe the Maasai would wish to join the Maasai who lived in northern Tanzania. The new nation would disintegrate before it even got off the drawing table.

Kenyatta told the Somali Members of Parliament that if the Somali people in Kenya wanted to be governed from the Somali government in Mogadishu, they could leave the

land and migrate to Somalia.
They agreed, and today north-
eastern Kenya is still part of Kenya,
and the country proudly has many
Kenyans who are from Somali
communities.

A few years later, another great
threat to the unity of the country
occurred. Kenya's Minister for
Economic Development, Tom
Mboya, was shot down on a
Nairobi street in 1969.

This event set off street battles
and mistrust between people all
over the country. Kenyatta appealed to all
Kenyan citizens not to destroy all that they had
achieved in building a strong, unified nation.

Kenyatta had to invoke his principle of unity
again and again. "Remember, we can only build
our country if we work together in the spirit of
harambee, pulling together with each other!" he
cried.

Kenyatta displayed the kind of vigour in the

running of the nation rarely manifested by a man of his age. He wanted to see Kenya grow into a united, powerful nation.

He initiated the construction of the Kenyatta International Conference Centre in Nairobi. This is one of the most magnificent buildings in Kenya.

"Our greatest enemies are poverty, disease and ignorance," he told a crowd of people. "We have to work hard to get rid of these things. *Uhuru na Kazi!* Freedom with hard work! Go to your farms and work hard!"

Kenyatta himself had to follow his own advice. He never wanted to get out of touch with the country, and many mornings he would spend hours working on his farm. He travelled on weekends to different parts of the country to visit rural villages, to keep in touch with agricultural growth, to open new schools.

"No Kenyan child should be denied the chance to go to school," he said. "We have to build enough schools for all our children." Not only were primary and secondary schools established, but Kenyatta University College was founded at this time to provide higher education for Kenyans.

Kenya's beautiful landscapes and wonderful animals attract people from all over the world. Kenyatta himself loved the National Parks in Kenya, and sometimes took his good friend, the Emperor Haile Selassie of Ethiopia, to a game park. The two would wander around among elephants and giraffes, chatting about the problems of running a whole country.

"They're magnificent animals, aren't they?" commented Selassie, nodding in the direction of a family of elephants.

"Yes, my friend," replied Kenyatta. "But I am very concerned about the increase in ivory trade."

"In fact," his friend replied, "poaching is becoming an international crisis. We should bring it up at the next meeting of the OAU."

The Organization for African Unity was established in May 1963 to allow all the African nations a chance to discuss issues with each other and find solutions which they could all agree on. Kenya joined officially after it had achieved independence.

"We also have to discuss the situation in southern Africa," added Selassie.

"Yes," agreed Kenyatta. "We cannot claim to be free, ourselves, as long as our brothers in Angola, Rhodesia and South Africa are under colonialism." At that time, these countries had not yet gained their own independence.

The two friends talked at length, while watching Kenya's beautiful animals. In the evening they watched traditional Kenyan dancing, another thing they both enjoyed.

Kenyatta was friends with Milton Obote, the president of Uganda, and Julius Nyerere, the

president of Tanzania. Together they
established the East African Community, to
strengthen the economies of the three East
African countries. During the time of the East
African Community, the three countries
prospered.

And so it was a painful experience for
Kenyatta when a military government in Uganda
threw out President Obote by force, and then
ruled the country badly. This led to the collapse
of the East African Community.

Equally depressing for Kenyatta was the news of the overthrow of his good friend Haile Selassie in 1974. Again, this was a forceful takeover by a junta, and this government of soldiers and guns also mismanaged the country.

Kenyatta believed strongly in the rule of law. He was convinced that the role of the military was only to protect its country from an outside enemy, not to govern the country inside its borders.

Kenyatta greatly respected his friend, Haile Selassie. One of the major streets in Nairobi is named after him in honour of his contribution to Kenya's independence.

CHAPTER TEN

THE LAST DAYS

 Kenyatta kept pursuing a busy schedule as leader of one of the most prosperous nations in Africa. Nevertheless, towards the end of his life Kenyatta had become very weak. While he had access to modern doctors, he was never far away from his grandfather's art of medicine. Whenever he felt weak, he would always turn to the herbal remedies he had learned from Kungu. But there came a time, finally, when the herbs could do nothing.

On the morning of the 21st of August, 1978 he was in Mombasa. Standing next to the First

Lady of the nation, Mama
Ngina, he awarded
honours to two of
Kenya's sporting
superstars, Henry Rono,
an Olympic runner, and
the boxer, Stephen
Muchoki. They each
received the "Order of the Burning Spear" from
their president.

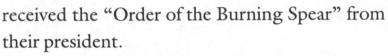

Kenyatta placed great value on the nation's
athletes, and delighted when they brought
honour to the country. Kenyan runners became
known all over the world, and the national
football team, the Harambee Stars, was one of
the strongest of the African teams.

"Your noble performance caused the Kenyan
National Anthem to be played in Edmonton,
Canada!" Kenyatta beamed with pride. "And
our flag was flown seven times over the games!"
He smiled and concluded, "I am very proud of
both of you."

Later that day, Kenyatta received Kenya's

ambassadors who were on their way to represent Kenya in foreign countries around the world.

In the evening, Kenyatta watched traditional Kenyan dancers with Mama Ngina sitting by his side, and then he retired early.

In the night, he turned in bed and looked into Mama Ngina's loving eyes. Mama Ngina was wide-awake.

"Any problem, *baba*?" she asked.

"Bring me some water," he replied.

Mama Ngina went to pour him a glass of water and brought it to him. After drinking the water, he sighed deeply. "Mama, is there anything I have not done?"

"No, you have done everything," Mama Ngina answered.

That night Kenyatta died peacefully in his sleep.

The next morning, the sad news swept across the country. Within hours, most towns were deserted. Shopkeepers closed their shops. Many offices closed. Everyone had gone home to mourn the loss of the Father of their nation.

Because Kenyatta was president of his nation, the new president had to take office immediately. There was an emergency meeting and the Vice-President, Daniel arap Moi, was sworn in as the new Acting President of Kenya.

Even when planning for his own death, Kenyatta had the unity of the nation foremost in his mind. He had to worry about how to leave the nation in good hands. He had to find someone who could hold the country together after he was gone. After much deliberation, he had felt that Daniel arap Moi was the best choice of someone who could keep the nation unified.

In his acceptance speech, the new President promised to follow Kenyatta's *nyayo*, his footsteps, in ensuring the unity of the country. "With the help of God, I will do my best to carry on with the work President Kenyatta had already started. I will devote myself to ensure the protection of every citizen and particularly small children who are the future leaders of this country."

The first big job of the new President was to preside over the funeral and burial of the first president, Jomo Kenyatta. President Moi led Kenyans through the mourning period peacefully, ensuring the unity of the nation which Kenyatta knew was so important.

Kenyans were given three days' leave to mourn their fallen leader. Thousands and thousands of mourners of all ages and from all walks of life went to State House in Nairobi to pay homage to their first president. They came from all over the country. In one day, 40,000 people moved slowly in a double line filed past Mzee's body to say goodbye. Many wept as they looked upon his face for one last time.

After people had had a chance to pay their last respects to their fallen hero, the burial took place. There was a magnificent parade that lasted all day. Kenyatta's body, lying on a great chariot, was transported from State House down the centre of Uhuru Highway to Parliament.

The burial was a formal ceremony within Parliament Grounds. A woman from the armed forces came forward in full uniform to represent all the armed forces. She laid a magnificent wreath of flowers on Kenyatta's grave.

Kenyatta was buried inside a special monument built in his memory. It stands in Parliament Grounds and if you visit Nairobi, you will see it there today.